Cute Animals
Coloring Book

Cute Animals
Coloring Book

Adorable creatures to color in

SIRIUS

SIRIUS

This edition published in 2022 by Sirius Publishing, a division of
Arcturus Publishing Limited,
26/27 Bickels Yard, 151–153 Bermondsey Street,
London SE1 3HA

ISBN: 978-1-3988-2227-6
CH007282NT
Supplier 29, Date 0662, Print run PI00001920

Printed in China

Created for children 10+

Introduction

Welcome to a menagerie of some of the most delightful animals you'll ever have a chance to color in. There are aardvarks and alpacas, tigers and turtles as well as a cute selection of animals pictured in their natural environments. Some are simple outlines; others have more detailed patterning for you to concentrate on.

Using either colored pencils or felt tip pens, use your judgement to decide on a color palette for each animal. You may select delicate pastels for some of these, while others may suggest a more vibrant scheme. Whatever you choose, you'll have hours of relaxing fun coloring in these charming creatures.

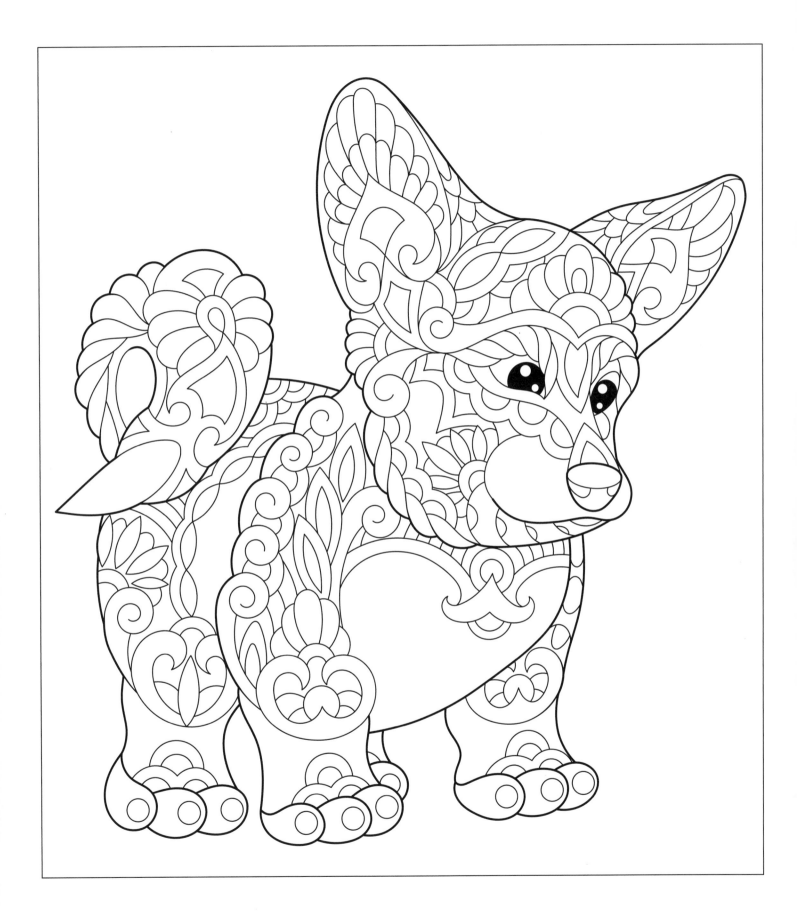

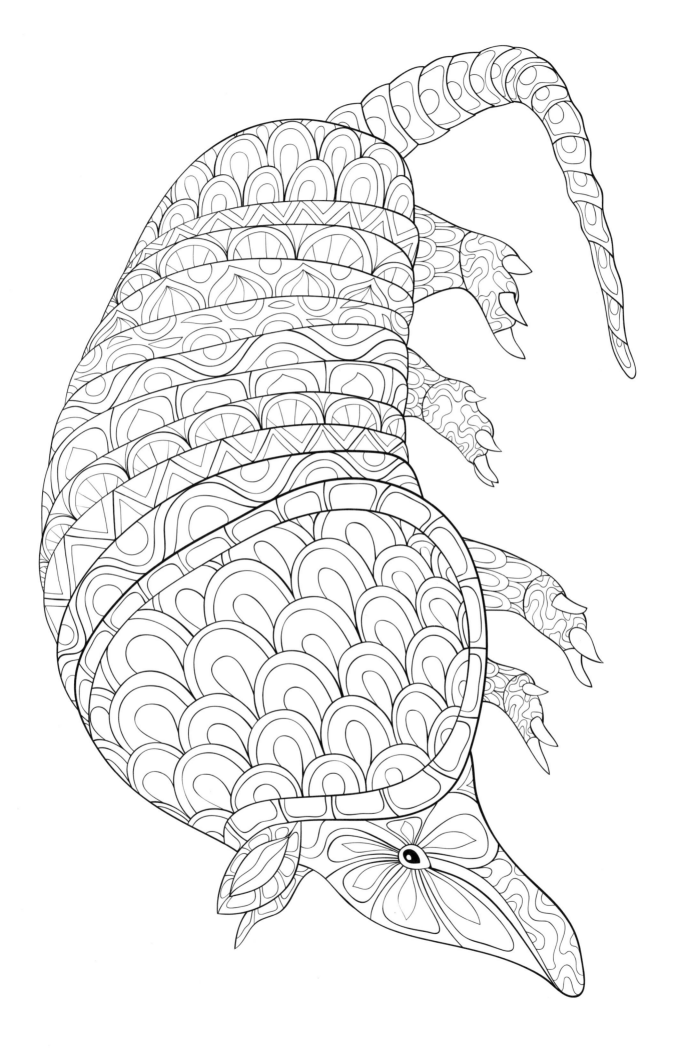

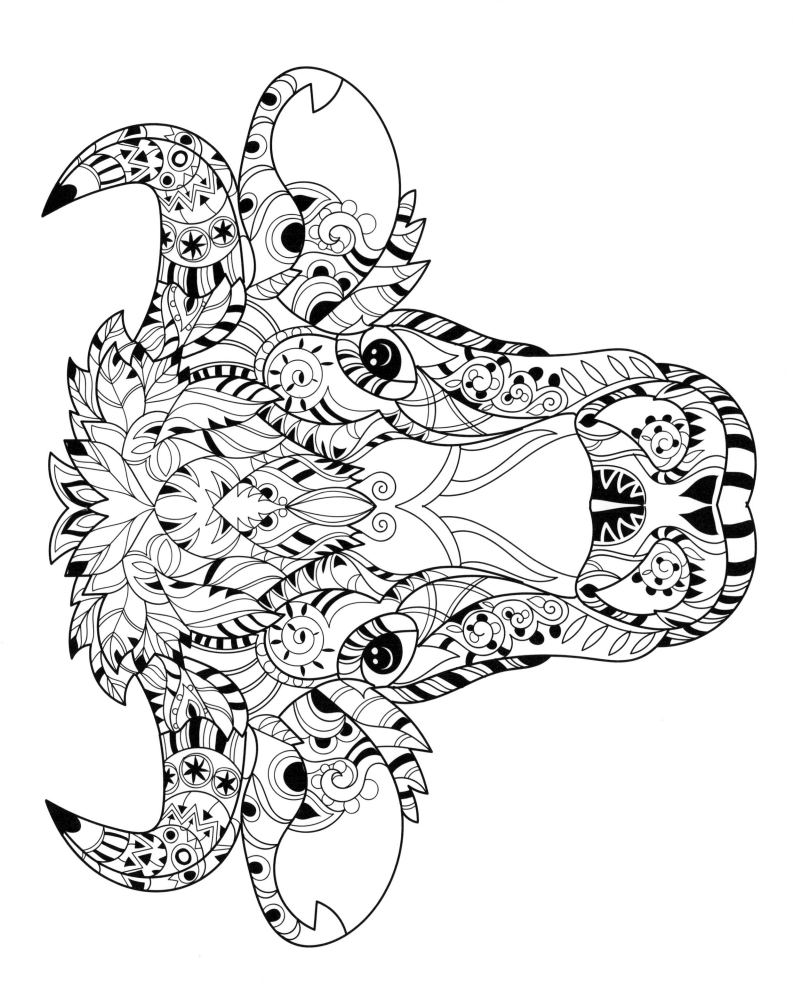

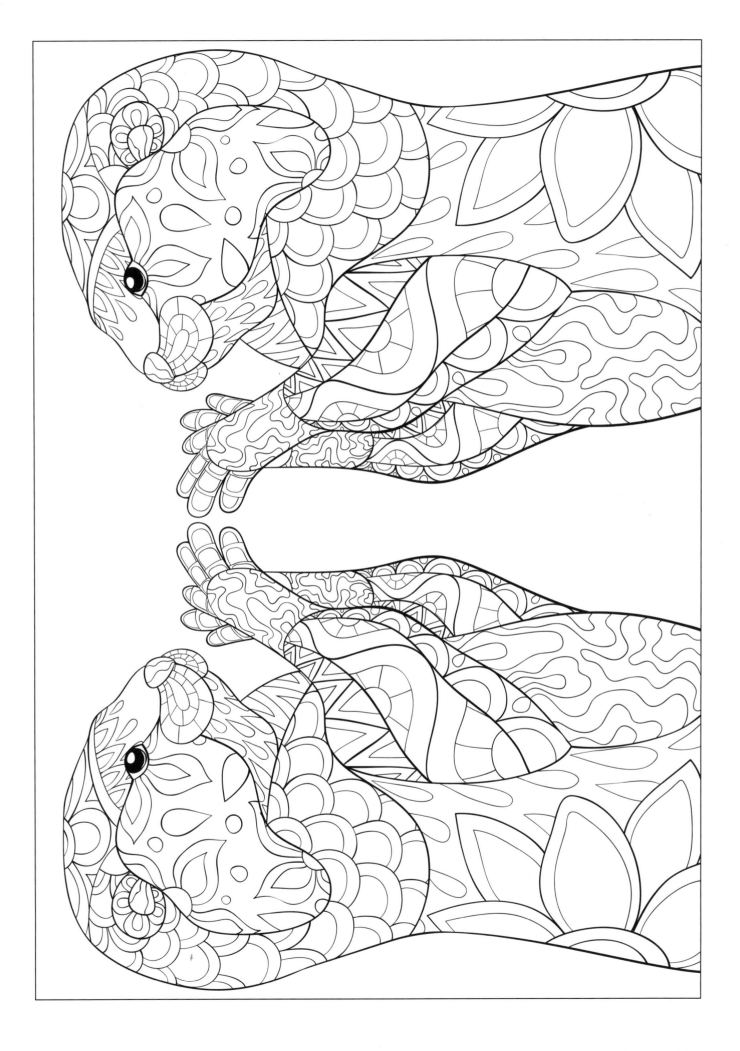

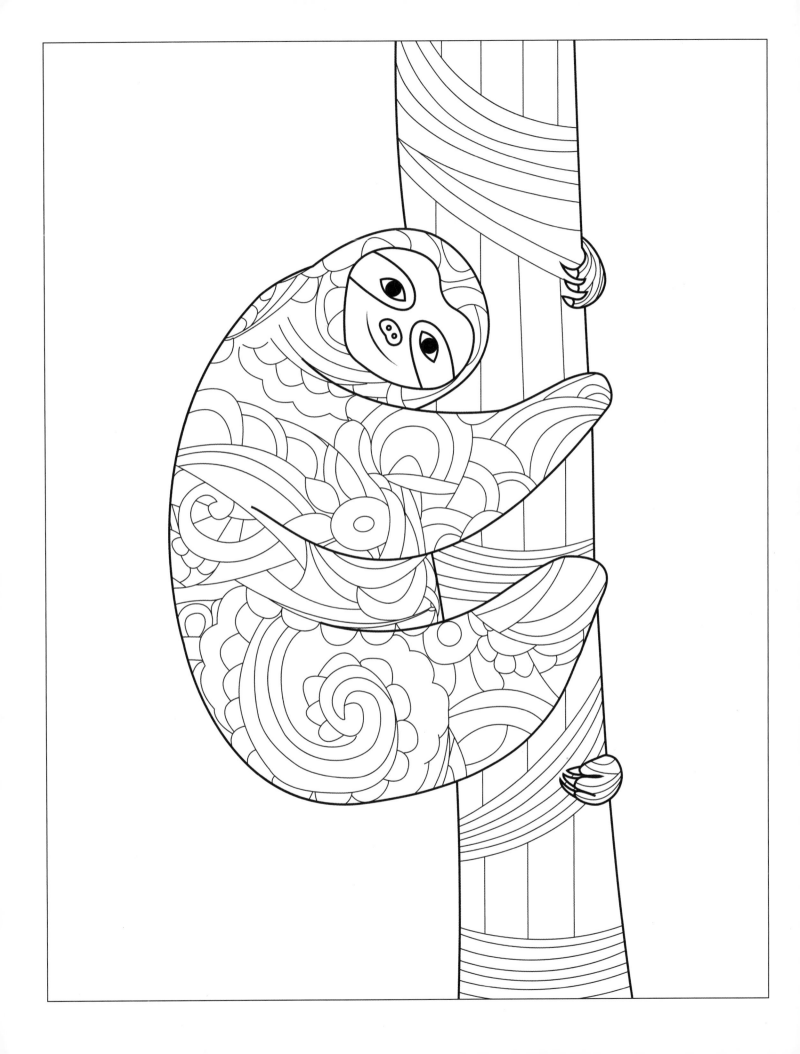

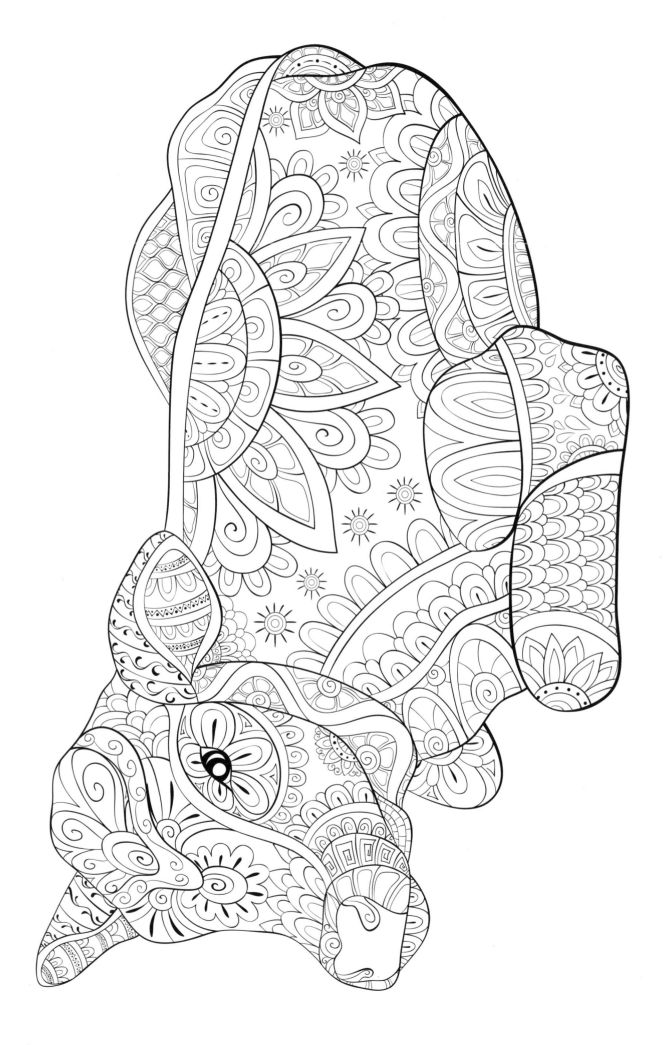

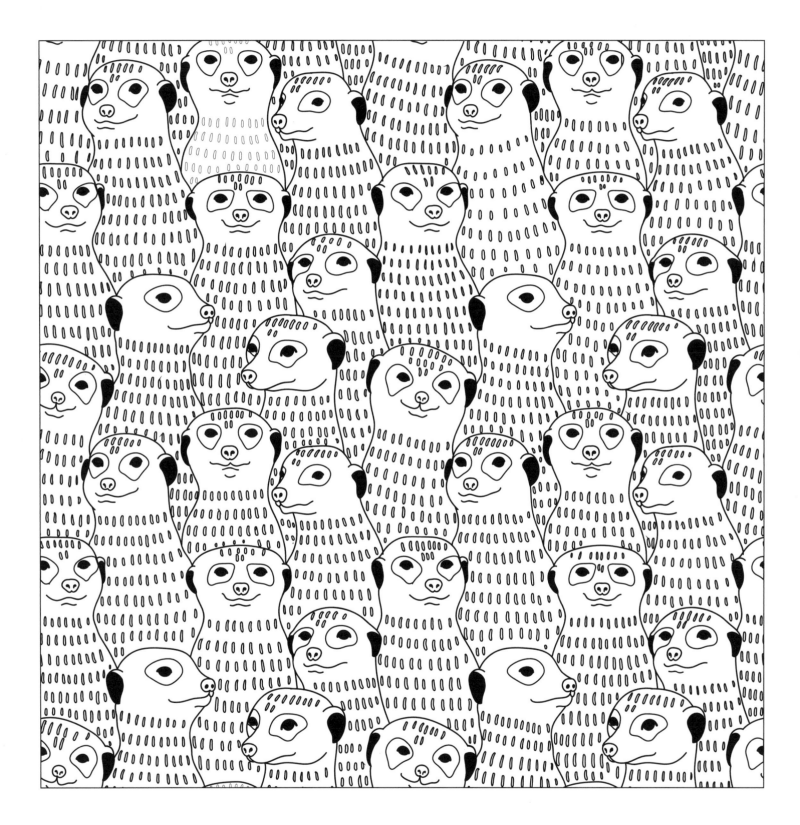

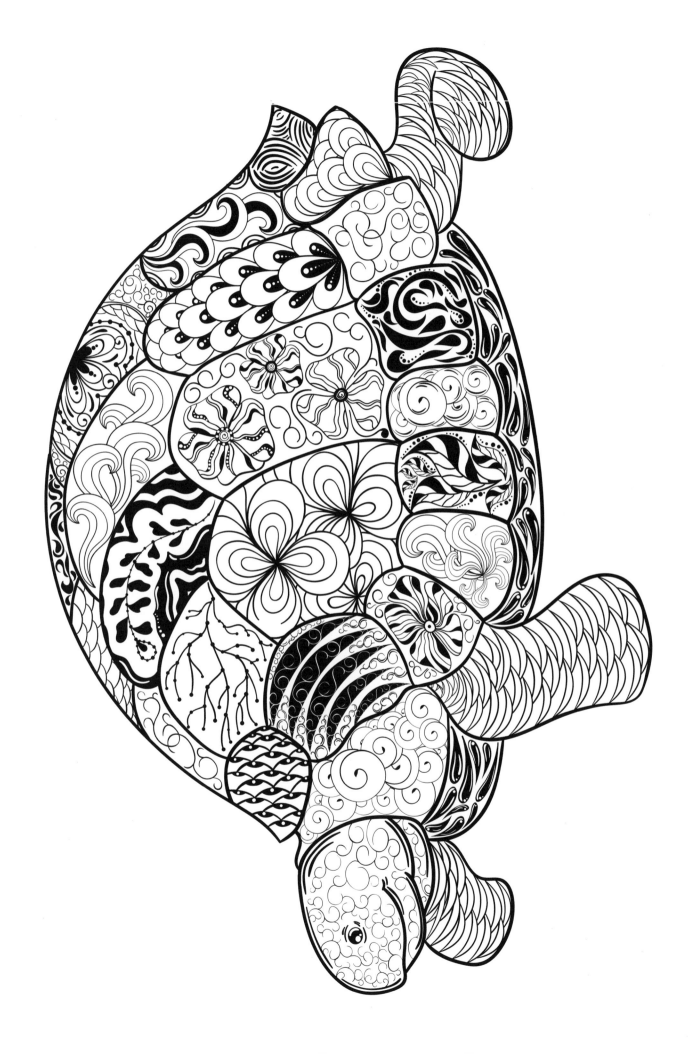